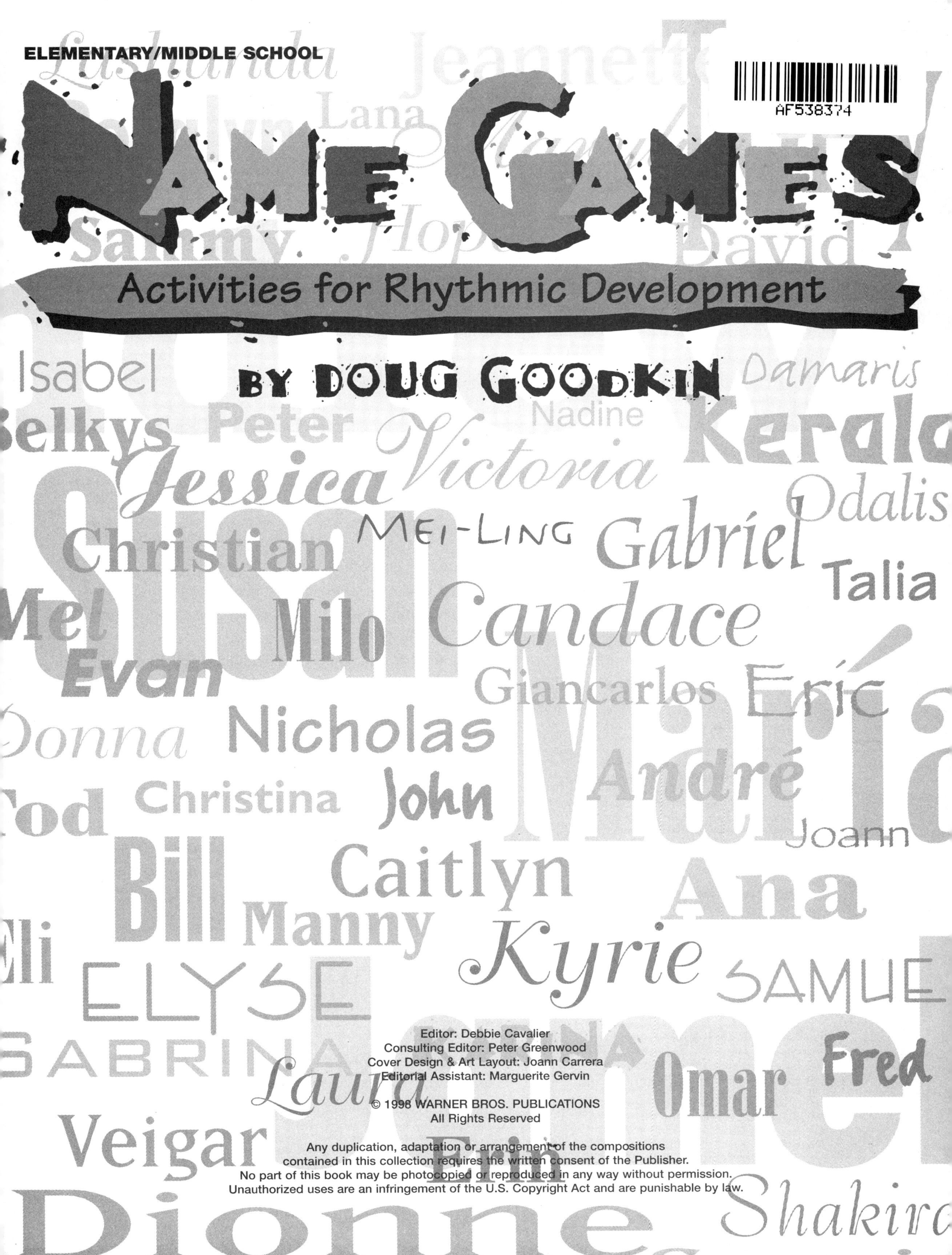

ELEMENTARY/MIDDLE SCHOOL

NAME GAMES

Activities for Rhythmic Development

BY DOUG GOODKIN

Editor: Debbie Cavalier
Consulting Editor: Peter Greenwood
Cover Design & Art Layout: Joann Carrera
Editorial Assistant: Marguerite Gervin

Preface

Our names carry so much. A rose by any other name may still be a rose, but had Bartholomew been named Butch, he would have been a different person. These tiny explosions of consonants and vowels speak of heroes, friends, family, and an entire ancestral line. We may be more than our name, but we are never less than it; we can cover it with clothes or wear it on our back, but it is tattooed forever into our skin.

First names first. Who were you named for? Tracing it back, you learn something about your parents. You discover their favorite aunts and uncles, old school chums, heroes and heroines from the movies, books, sports, and arts. You enter the thinking of Mom and Dad and reveal something of their character. Were they whimsical? "We named you Jasmine because we were under a trellis of that fragrant flower when we first kissed." Traditional? "My father was George, his father was George, and I want my grandson to be George." Inventive? "Because you are a blend of us, Joe and Donna, we named you Joeonna. "Boring? "You're Sally because it was the most popular name at that time." Alliterative? "We thought Frederick Frederickson flowed nicely." Humorous (and perhaps a bit cruel)? "With a last name like Kent, Clark was just too good to resist."

Nicknames. If first names carry the past of our parents forward to the future—the character they might wish for us—nicknames speak of our character as it unfolds over time. We are given our first name by parents, but our nickname tells who we are in our community of family and friends, changing through time as our relationships change. To his mother, he is Jonathan; to his childhood friends, Johnny; to his colleagues, John; to his drinking buddies, Johnster; to his wife, John darling. Nicknames speak of affection (my daughter Kerala became "Ker bear") or ridicule (my wife, Karen, and her brother, Barclay, were "Carrot and Broccoli"), and sometimes both at once (Louis Armstrong's derogatory nickname "Satchelmouth" became the endearing "Satchmo").

The best nicknames reveal informally what other cultures practice formally. Native American Jamake Highwater writes:

> *One of the most significant features of Indian tribal custom is the giving of individuated names. Such Indian names denote personal qualities, heroic exploits, uncommon abilities, unique physical characteristics, visionary experiences, and other designations that point specifically to the singularity of the person being named . . . every North American Indian is given, in a tribal ceremony, a name that recognizes his uniqueness.*

From that tradition, we find Rolling Thunder, Sitting Bull, Crazy Horse—names that connect with the natural world. From another tradition, one of informal initiation, we find the jazz royalty of Duke, Count, Prez, King, and Lady Day.

Other people give us nicknames, but we may change our given names to announce a new identity. Our motivation may be religious: Richard Alpert became Baba Ram Dass, and Cassius Clay became Mohammed Ali. We may try to *conceal* our identity by dropping the "stein" in Goldstein, or we may create a popular persona with a new name the way Roy Scherer Jr. (Rock Hudson), or Annie Mae Bullock (Tina Turner) did. By changing our name, we take a step out of our given identity towards our chosen one.

Middle names. An opportunity to preserve a family name (John Beswick Shultz), a second chance to honor someone (we named our daughter Talia Jane Goodkin for my wife's college friend), or a security blanket in case the first names don't fit (my father, wife, and brother-in-law all chose to be known by their middle names). Middle names also help distinguish two people with similar names—John Smith from John Jacob Jingleheimer Smith.

Last names. To some people, a surname proclaims ethnic identity and conjures up ancestors. To others, it tells a very different story. For example, African-Americans lost their ancestral names when they were enslaved and renamed by their oppressors, and women often relinquish their family name when they marry. Bill Bryson reports in his book, *Mother Tongue,* that last names in England were at one time less fixed. When an English poll tax was passed in 1379, the government required a census of names. To distinguish one Peter from another, Peter Johnson (Peter, son of John) and Peter Robertson were created.

Patriarchy was not the only source of surnames. Some came from occupations: Smith, Carpenter, Miller, Weaver, Singer, Harper, Cook, Taylor, Shearer, Shepherd, Hunter; while others came from nicknames: Armstrong, Whitehead, Richman, Redman.

Place was a significant part of identity in more stable cultures and gave us names like St. Francis of Assisi, Hildegard von Bingen, and Leonardo da Vinci. (Nowadays, "Doug of New Jersey" doesn't have quite the same ring.) Some surnames refer to a landmark: Wells, Bush, Stone, Bridges.

Time also enters into the naming process in some cultures. The Akan people of West Africa mark the day of the week a child is born—a boy born on Sunday is named Kwasi, a girl, Akosuwa. In Spain, children are named for the patron saint of their birth date, either directly (José) or indirectly (María-José). In Bali, it is the birth order that counts—Wayan means the first born male, Made, the second, and so on. (I often wonder what it must be like to teach there—"Wayan, pay attention!" would bring half the class to order!)

A journey into names is an exploration of past, present, and future, as well as a glimpse of family, ancestors, culture, place, and time. It tells a bit of who we are by revealing where we came from. By sharing that journey, and telling our stories, we begin to know each other and feel known in a special way. The 20 name games presented here can be the first step on that journey.

Contents

Introduction

Each one has a name, some are short, some are long.
When you put them all together, it's a song.

Avon Gillespie, my first Orff teacher, often began his classes with that little chant. The words are simple, but the message profound: In this class, the unique *you* is one note in the polyphony of the group *we*. Our song, shaped from the elemental material of word and gesture, will grow from the joining of our individual selves. The alchemy of this approach creates the gold of aesthetic expression from the base metal of simple elements. The experiment begins with a single spoken word—our name.

Every music teacher uses name games, and each has his or her own favorite game. Even those of us who rove from class to class teaching hundreds of children attempt to learn the names of our students. On a personal level, we indeed want to get to know each of them and on a philosophical level, we want each of them to feel known. Knowing their names is a starting point for both. On a practical level, a name is a powerful method of control—"Gerry!" will get a better result than "Hey, you!"

As music (and movement) specialists, everything we do in class should overflow with musicality—the means should support the ends. If we are to learn each other's names in music class, how can we do it in a musical way? How can the process help teach the skills and concepts of our subject? How can we set the tone for all succeeding classes? How can we directly involve the children in their own learning? The games herein are 20 different answers to these questions.

These games grew out of many years of teaching both children and adults. Each game has its own little story, arising from a particular need. As I put them in order for this collection, I was delighted to see an overall pattern naturally emerge. What seemed at first to be an interesting way to learn students' names grew to a full-blown approach for developing musicality and musical understanding. These games reveal many of the principles of Orff-Schulwerk—its expressive media, its unique path to rhythmic development, its organic approach to composition, and its model of communal learning. Those already versed in this approach may find familiar processes aimed in new directions; those new to it may be intrigued by its imaginative pedagogy. In either case, it may be helpful to consider how these principles come alive in these name games.

Expressive Media

Orff-Schulwerk begins with that which is closest to us—the various sounds, gestures, and movements of our bodies in combination with the sounds, speech, and song of our voices. All of these games begin in the body and voice and so require nothing more than a group of people, a space to work in, and an active imagination. This democratic approach makes the material equally accessible to teachers of all subjects and music programs of all economic levels.

Because the games are based on *ideas* rather than repertoire for specific instruments, all of the material may be extended to any combination of instruments. The Orff music class generally uses a variety of unpitched percussion and xylophones, but the same pieces transferred to school supplies (paper struck with a pencil, a ruler twanged on the edge of a desk, and a pen scraping the edge of a spiral notebook), band instruments (tubas, trumpets, and saxophones), or orchestral instruments (violins, cellos, and flutes) will enliven any class.

Rhythmic Development

"The speech exercise comes at the beginning of all musical practice," according to Carl Orff and his collaborator Gunild Keetman, and these games follow that path to rhythmic competency. Experiences in steady beat, tempo, meter, duration, accent, phrasing, ostinati, polyrhythm, and other rhythmic elements help develop the child's innate rhythmic sense. Some children come to music class with a rhythmicity learned in the womb and in their first few years of life; others may have missed out on the rhythmic lessons that nursing, knee-bouncing, and rhyme chanting teach. But whether it's building from a solid rhythmic base or remediating missed opportunities, the repetition in these games helps teach what some think is unteachable—a sense of rhythm.

Composition

One of the best questions I was ever asked at a workshop came after we played a name game. "Is that a piece or an exercise?" My answer was, "Yes." Each activity presented here might be called an exercise because it is designed for a specific end, i.e., learning people's names or warming up the group. Yet it also should have the quality of a piece, with a clear beginning, middle, and end. Whether we enjoy them as a one-time activity or decide to follow the ideas that emerge and work them into a full-blown composition, we should aim for a sense of musical performance. We begin with a moment of expectant silence and focused state of readiness, keep the energy moving through all the transitions and end with another, markedly different, moment of silence before relaxing. Regardless of the content, we have lived a musical piece, a journey in sound framed at each end.

With this approach, the students are present for every step in the building of the composition. They can see it emerge from the seed of a single idea and watch how it grows, watered by their collective contributions. The result may not be as pleasing as a piece from a master composer, but what it lacks in sophistication, it makes up for in involvement. Instead of imitating the *result* of a composer's creative process, it allows students to get inside that process itself, to begin to think and hear as a composer, but at their own level.

Such an approach also provides an entry point into the repertoire of existing compositions. Exploring the variations of timbre in clapping, snapping, and patting names opens a door to orchestration. The upbeats in the name Isabel lead us to the rhythm of the "William Tell Overture" and the name Kamila helps us learn the jazz ride cymbal pattern. Spelling names opens the door to mixed meters while the various games with simultaneous ostinati prepare us for the polyrhythmic texture of most music. What seems at first like a mere "warm-up" activity soon shifts to the center, opening up a marvelous musical world just right for each developmental stage of the child.

Community Building
Music has always served a community function. Kids playing ring games, clapping hand-jive, and jumping rope while chanting are actively engaged in the trials and errors of socialization; kids singing in the church or school choir get practice in the rewards and difficulties of group endeavors; kids playing in the school or neighborhood band are learning further lessons—come on time, tune your instrument with the others, learn how your part fits in with the whole. Nowadays these experiences are endangered. TV, the Internet, video games, and adult-organized competitive sports have largely replaced the old neighborhood children's culture. As teachers encounter an ever-growing number of students lacking basic social and emotional skills once taken for granted, we will see the rise of more and more techniques for remediating the loss of social intelligence. Yet most will be contrived and artificial compared to the tried-and-true practice of music-making.

These games help develop community not only by singing, dancing, and playing together, but by *creating* together in each of these mediums. The difficulties and victories of co-creation enhance the community effort by bringing aesthetics into the process—when we make something beautiful together, we rise to a new level. *

Children need these activities more than ever. We may not be able to revive the old neighborhood children's culture, but we can bring a bit of its spirit into the classroom. Though these games are adult-supervised, they bring an attentive ear to the child's world.

Adults likewise need these experiences. Though these games came from and are offered back to the children in the music classroom, they are equally relevant to the business team-building workshop, the New Age drum circle, the school parent meeting, and just plain old neighborhood get-togethers. We all want to be named and be known, to sing, dance, play, and create together.

* Our school staff recently took a Ropes Course, one of many team-building remedial methods. We were given the group task of creating two overlapping squares of rope on the ground while blindfolded. After twenty long minutes of arguing, laughing, and shouting, we removed the blindfolds and looked at the ropes. After my initial reaction of surprise, I thought, "All that work for this?!" The process was the same as collectively creating a piece of music, but the *product* was distinctly different—in one case, two pieces of rope, in the other, a beautiful piece of music.

How to use this Book

Formation
The games herein are played in a circle, seated or standing, unless otherwise noted. To "take turns" means to go around the circle one at a time.

Age Level
These games are adaptable across all age levels. In general, the games proceed from simple to complex. Activities for the very young (two–six years old) need to be simple, in unison (not parts), and taught by aural imitation. Activities dependent on multiple parts and notation are best reserved for ages seven and up. I've resisted designating age groups for the games because there are so many variables. The children will clearly communicate by their energy level whether a game is too easy or too hard and you can adjust accordingly.

Sequential Development
This potpourri of games is not a precisely ordered curriculum, but it is arranged so that anyone ambitious enough to play them all would discover a progression. Those interested in trying a number of games might consider a different one for each age level (a good way to prepare for the final activity, "Rumpelstiltskin").

Class Size
Games that require a response from each student—saying names one at a time—usually reach a critical mass at 15 or so students; kids get restless, interest wanes. For larger groups (say 30), you may choose to form two groups, one for the beginning of class and one for the end. Some games may be played in more than one group simultaneously once the principle has been demonstrated and understood. Older children, who have made the connection between speech and rhythm and can hold their own parts amidst many layers, can go directly to games that require simultaneous expression or that move quickly around the circle.

Skills
The skills listed at the beginning of each game indicate which are required for successful playing and which can be developed through repeated playing. They also serve as a list of symptoms that help you diagnose problems. Do the children need more work with steady beat? Are they having trouble tracking? Can they hear it but lack the physical coordination to express it or do they have the motor skills, but lack aural comprehension? After playing the games, have a discussion about the skills employed. Affirming your students' improvements and recognizing their next challenge helps them become more aware of their learning process.

Concepts
The question of which game to play can be answered partly by the concept it highlights. If your class is learning basic note values, the games emphasizing syllables serve well; if the focus is meter, the spelling game can demonstrate the grouping of beats. Like skills, the concepts are markers on the musical path that help students see their progress.

Classroom Adaptations
Classroom teachers may use these games with a different conceptual emphasis—defining syllables, substituting spelling words for names, graphing math patterns, teaching alliteration in poetry, discussing origins of names. (Music teachers, share this book with your classroom colleagues!) How exciting it would be for the child to play the same game in math class, language arts class, history class, and music class with each teacher highlighting a different aspect—a truly integrated curriculum.

GAME 1. NAME RHYTHM

Skills: Hearing the natural spoken rhythm of each name
Matching speech and body percussion
Imitating leader's expression
Sensing the ending

Concepts: Duration values
Upbeats

Activities:

- Speak and clap your own name to a steady beat and invite the group to join you. Cue the end with gesture or inflection (louder, softer, hi-low, etc.):

Doug, Doug, Doug, Doug, Doug, Doug, ***Doug!***

- As above, speaking and clapping the name of the next child in the circle:

Jen-ny, Jen-ny, Jen-ny, Jen-ny, Jen-ny, Jen-ny, ***Jen-ny!***

- Continue around the circle until all names have been recited.

Variations:

- Perform with various body percussion (pat knees, snap fingers, etc.)
- Perform with gestures.
- Perform with different voice qualities.
- Have students suggest ways to perform each other's names.
- Have students create their own ways to express their names.

Comments:

This is the game I use to begin my first class with three-year-olds. It introduces the children to the basic mediums of beginning music class—body percussion, expressive speech, song, and gesture—and sets the tone for future classes by taking a musical approach to a concrete task—learning names. Repeating the names and hooking them to rhythm and gesture helps us all learn and remember them. We also make our first vital connection between the syllables of names and the basic rhythmic values of music. From John comes ♩ and from Sally ♫ . If Sophia is in class, three-year-olds begin to get a feeling for upbeats— 𝅘𝅥𝅯 ♬ .

Being masters at mimicry, most three-year-olds join in right away—but not all. Some sit there dumbfounded, wondering what they've gotten themselves into. Some are shy about hearing their name so forcefully and publicly pronounced, while others are tickled to be offered such recognition. Not only will you learn the children's names, but also something of their personalities.

This beginning game works well with most any age, though I wouldn't recommend it as a starting activity for teenagers.

Game 2. Name Phrases

Skills: Keeping a steady beat
Internalizing a word while expressing rhythm (audiation)
Following a rhythmic sequence

Concepts: Rhythm and beat
Anacrusis (upbeat)
Rhythmic phrasing

Activities:

- Once students' names are known, all clap each student's name four times going around the circle, keeping a steady beat:

Tom Tom Tom Tom Jes-si-ca Jes-si-ca Jes-si-ca Jes-si-ca Lin-da Lin-da Lin-da Lin-da

- Repeat as above, saying each name silently (audiation) while clapping.
- As above, three times per name.
- As above, twice per name.
- As above, once per name.

Variations:

- Go around the circle in the opposite direction.
- Start at a different point in the circle.
- Divide group in two, each going in the opposite direction.
- All find their own starting point and perform simultaneously.
- All close eyes and perform by memory.
- Arrange people to create an intentional rhythmic flow, with attention to contrast, repetition, and cadence.

Comments:

This game extends the skills and concepts of our first game by grouping the names and reciting them in a continuous flow. The contrast between names of different syllables becomes sharper and the relationship between name rhythms and steady beat becomes clearer. It also clarifies which names start on the beat and which have a natural accent before the beat (anacrusis). Sylvia, Maria, and Isabel all have three syllables, but begin at a different moment in relation to the beat: Sylvia- Maria- Isabel-

Setting the names in patterns reinforces the idea of rhythmic phrasing. The "fourness" so characteristic of much Western music is a good starting point, but from the beginning it can be balanced by the "threes" and "twos" of the variations.

This exercise also introduces the idea of internalizing words, sometimes (and herein) called *audiation*. This is an important exercise for "bringing the music inside" and reoccurs throughout these games.

Here we introduce the concept of notation, but instead of black marks on paper, *we* are the notation. Each child represents the rhythm of his or her name as we shift our focus around the circle. The eyes-closed variation is particularly powerful—not only do we internalize the music through audiation, but we internalize *each other* as we visualize each face while clapping.

An observer unaware of our notation system would be impressed by a group of young children clapping such a complicated pattern. How does the whole group know when to change together? How could they have learned it in five to ten minutes? Our secret is simple—the circle gives us the form for our score and our names provides the rhythmic content, awakening the ancient connection between speech and rhythm.

Game 3. Layering Name Rhythms

Skill: Maintaining one's part in a multi-layered rhythmic texture

Concepts: Complementary rhythms
Timbre
Diminishing pattern

Activities:

- Teacher claps his/her own name four times. Next person enters following the established beat while teacher keeps clapping his/her name. Continue around the circle until all have entered:

- All continue expressing rhythm of name by snapping fingers.
- As above, patting knees, stamping, or patting floor.
- Four times at each level—snap, clap, pat, stamp.
- As above, three times at each level, then twice, and once.
- All choose own pattern of snaps, claps, pats, stamps.

Variations:

- Speak name four times, play four times (choose one option above).

- As above, creating a pattern.

  speak 4, play 4, speak 3, play 3, speak 2, play 2, speak 1, play 1.

Comments:

While GAME 2 concentrates on a single rhythmic expression of one name at a time around the circle, this game introduces a polyrhythm of many name rhythms simultaneously. I reserve this for first graders and older, ages when such layering is not only possible but also meaningful for the children. Many newcomers to Orff are impressed by the children's ability to stay together in ensemble pieces and it is exercises like these that develop the ability to hear how one's part fits into the total mosaic. Once again, language aids us in keeping our part steady in a multi-layered rhythmic texture, a skill vital to samba bands and string quartets alike.

This teaching approach is usually reserved for young children, but a college class surveying cross-cultural music might do well to begin with this activity as an introduction to the polyrhythmic layers of a West African drum ensemble. Our previous name game might be an excellent springboard to the monorhythmic variations of North Indian tabla drumming. Keeping music connected to the body and the imagination and the group experience is a good idea at every stage of our musical training.

Game 4. Layering Name Rhythms—Extensions

Skills: Maintaining one's part in a polyrhythmic texture
Simultaneous imitation

Concepts: Complementary rhythms
Timbre

Activities:

- All speak names simultaneously to a steady beat (as in previous game).
- Maintain rhythm vocally with the sound "ch." Change to other mouth sounds: tongue clicks, "scat" syllables.
- Sing name on one pitch, changing at leader's cue. Next sing on two pitches, then three.
- Maintain rhythm with a gesture or a movement in place.
- Maintain rhythm with locomotive movement (walk, jump, crawl, etc.).
- All choose one of the above and perform simultaneously.
- Each maintains his or her own rhythm while watching another performer. At signal, switch and perform the rhythm and medium of the person watched.

Variation:

- Half the group performs, the other half watches. Switch.

Comments:

Rhythm lives in the voice through sound and is expressed in the body through gestures and movement. We are building our rhythmic vocabulary in GAMES 1–4 to include these expressive mediums. We might imagine different areas of the musical brain lighting up when rhythm sounds in the voice, or expresses itself by moving the shoulders and walking around the room. When one rhythm passes through a multitude of media, we have a deeper connection with our innate rhythmicity. Many cultures support this notion by teaching dances to drummers and drum rhythms through various vocal devices—poems, formal mnemonics, or informal imitation of instruments.*

This game introduces a handy pedagogical tool that can be revisited in any number of games and exercises—watching another's pattern while performing one's own and then imitating that idea at the leader's cue. This is, of course, quite difficult to do accurately, and requires a high level of concentration. Yet it is well worth the effort because it offers several things:

- An opportunity for each child to contribute her or his ideas and have them amplified by the group.
- An expanded base of ideas to imitate, more varied than any teacher could imagine.
- Recognition of the many levels of music learning: hearing and seeing other parts while playing our own.

* Play a recording of the Cuban group *Vocal Sampling* for a wonderful listening extension of percussive vocal sounds.

GAME 5. SYLLABLE GROUPING

Skills: Hearing a specific part in a dense texture
Transferring body percussion to unpitched percussion

Concepts: Duration values
Rhythmic accent

Activities:

- Form a circle. Select a name with one syllable to set the fundamental beat. Then have everyone clap the natural rhythm of their own names simultaneously. Two syllable names may be expressed as Lin-da ♫ or Linda ♫ 𝄾. The latter is more natural, but the former has a useful pedagogical function, leading us toward our later goal of notating quarter and eighth notes. (See GAME 13.)

- Have everyone walk into the middle of the circle while clapping and find someone else who is clapping the same rhythm. People who are "one of a kind" search for other "one of a kinds" and group together. Stay with the new group and reform the original circle. A sample group might look like this:

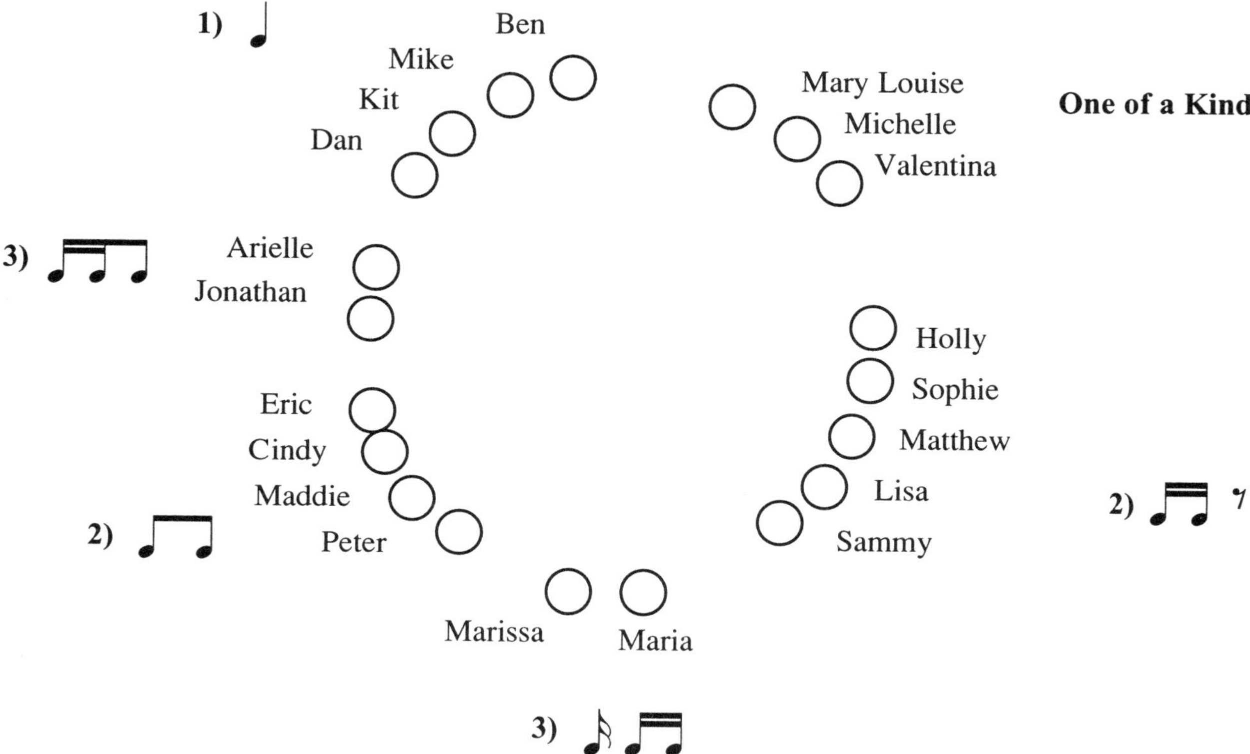

- Each group claps its rhythm four times to make sure each person is in the correct group.

- Each group performs a short improvisation based on its rhythm. The improvisation must have a clear beginning (one person starts), a middle (succeeding parts related to the opening statement and to each other), and an ending (decided non-verbally through attentive listening).

Variations:

- Each group chooses one type of percussion instrument (drum, shaker, wood, etc.) Repeat improvisation with instruments.

- One group plays its rhythm as an ostinato, the next group enters with its rhythm, and so on around the circle. A volunteer goes into the center and improvises on a different percussion instrument (temple blocks, conga drums, drum set, etc.).

Comments:

The idea for this game came from a workshop I led on building community and has served me faithfully ever since. Orff-Schulwerk not only effectively develops fundamental musical skills and understanding, but contributes to the growth of other intelligences as well, not the least of which is social. Making music is a unique way for people to be together, but *how* we make music together determines the quality of our experience. When play and creativity are mixed, something happens to a group of people—armor drops, social tension eases, good humor arises, and ideas begin to flow. For children, this is nothing special, simply an affirmation of the way they learn. When we play this game in my adult workshops, people feel like they're meeting a forgotten part of themselves—how delicious to *play* again!

The root idea of searching for one's own group can be applied to any number of other musical exercises. The basic format, in order of steps, is as follows (my commentary in italics):

1. Express something specific (in this case, the rhythm of one's name).

   Share something unique and distinct about your personality. Each of us longs to be known by the group and in turn to offer our gifts to the group. I tell my students that I hope they will stand out in my class and let their essence shine. Whether it be improvising a melody, contributing an idea, or creating a dance, children need an outlet to reveal themselves.

2. Find a "mate" in the midst of a crowd—one that has the same expression. ("One of a kinds" find other "one of a kinds" and form their own group.)

   Everyone belongs to some group. Although we are all unique, a piece of us is held in common with others. Each of us needs to feel that we belong to a community and that we are part of a greater whole. I also tell my students that I hope they will learn to "blend in" whether it be singing or dancing in unison, letting go of an idea in the group creative process, or adjusting their dynamic level in an ensemble piece. By balancing "stand out" and "blend in," we avoid selfish independence or sheepish conformity and we begin to understand when each is appropriate.

3. Return to the large group firmly established in one's sub-group.

   The sub-groups should not compete against other sub-groups, but feel themselves as part of a greater whole.

4. Solidify the sub-group by creating something together.

   Community moves from noun to verb when the group has actively worked and played together. Once established, the group must earn its identity; creating together is one of the most effective means to build community.

5. Solidify the large group by sharing.

   Creation is not complete until it is brought back and offered to the larger group.

6. Everyone belongs to more than one group. (The groups will change as we apply this form to other unifying concepts; e.g., the first sound of a name.)

   Duke Ellington was once asked by a reporter whether a composition of his was written for "his people." Without missing a beat, the quick-witted Ellington replied: "Which people do you mean? The Beajoulais drinkers? The Washington, D.C. folks? The people over 40?"

In addition to the important social metaphors of this game, there are a number of other levels operating. The ability to filter out distracting input and keep focused on the task by tuning the ear to a particular rhythm amidst the cacophony of many rhythms (both maddening and exhilarating!) is a crucial life skill, especially in our modern age of sensory and information overload.

Finally, the form of the improvisation is one that will serve us in many different exercises. When we improvise without any pre-planning or prior discussion, we set the stage for trusting our impulses—"first thought = best thought"—and sharpening our listening. This approach will come up later in group composition when we begin by *doing* rather than *thinking*.

GAME 6. SYLLABLE GROUPING—EXTENSIONS

Skills: Associative memory
Grouping (chunking)

Concept: Duration values

Activities:

- Form groups by rhythm as in GAME 5. Go around the circle one group at a time. Each person in the group says his or her name in order, and the entire group repeats the sequence of names: Ben: "Ben"; Mike: "Mike"; Kit: "Kit"; Dan: "Dan"; whole group: "Ben, Mike, Kit, Dan." If a group is larger than five, divide it into groups of three, four, or five.

- Continue as above with the next group ("Arielle, Jonathan"). Repeat from the beginning and continue through the second group: "Ben, Mike, Kit, Dan, Arielle, Jonathan." Continue until the entire circle is memorized.

- After all names are memorized, clap name rhythms around circle while saying the name silently (audiation).

Variations:

- Speaking or clapping, go the other way around the circle.

- Leader silently chooses a starting point and starts clapping names around the circle. Group guesses starting point, based on the changes of rhythm:

Here is an example from the circle in GAME 5, going counterclockwise.

(Answer: Cindy)

- All choose starting point and a direction and clap simultaneously. All should end at the same time.

Comments:

I have played this game with groups as large as 35, and when I say I think we can memorize everyone's name within 10 minutes, most people shake their heads in disbelief. Little do they know the power of "associative memory" and "chunking"! Associative memory, which we use in GAME 2, is the learning specialist's term for anchoring memory through association—by sight, sound, rhythm, smell, corresponding word, or other possible hooks. The more entry points for memory, the better our chance of recall. Finding our place in the alphabet by singing "The ABC Song" is a perfect example of this process at work (and an affirmation of the importance of music in the learning process). In this game, we have a dual association: the rhythm of the word and the face of the person.

"Chunking" is the horrible word learning specialists have chosen for grouping things in units small enough to feel as a whole. The musical term (and more musical word) for that unit is "phrase." If we had to memorize each name and face in the circle individually, it would be as difficult as memorizing a melody one note at a time. We experienced some "chunking" in GAME 2 by repeating each name four times. Here memorizing all the one syllable names before proceeding to the two syllables seals the names in our memory. Cycling back through each unit before proceeding to the next further imbeds the information.

Once again, the group serves as a living score and the simple variations—going in the other direction or starting in a different place—create a new piece each time with relatively little effort.

Game 7: Positive and Negative

Skills: Internalizing one part while playing another
Improvising complementary patterns

Concepts: Complementary rhythms
Sound/silence interplay

Activities:

- All speak their own name and create an accompanying complementary pattern to a steady beat. The pattern cannot "touch" the name—speaking and clapping must complement each other, creating two distinctly different rhythms. In contrast to our previous games, this game invites us to vary the natural speech rhythm of our name:

- All express simultaneously, both speaking and clapping.

- Drop out clapping, continue speaking (leave rests for clapping part):

• Drop out speaking, continue clapping (leave rests for speaking part):

• Half the group only speaks, other half only claps.

Variations:

• Sing instead of speaking, move instead of clapping.

• Substitute percussion instruments for clapping, recorders/xylophones for speaking part.

• Create small group pieces based on above choices.

Comments:

This activity can be introduced (or reinforced) by showing pictures of two classic optical illusions—one which can be seen as either two facial profiles or a vase, another in which we see either an old woman or a young woman. Filling the space between syllables is an aural equivalent of that visual experience of positive and negative space, but with a markedly different purpose—to develop an aesthetic sensibility. The simple act of eliminating the clapping creates a group piece that has more room to breathe and a more varied texture than the preceding games; eliminating the speaking creates a different piece.

Getting a feel for the interplay between sound and silence is vital to the art of making music. In a jazz ensemble, the players listen intently for the space in the soloist's phrasing, making instant decisions about how to fill it; the symphonic composer must carefully place each sound with sensitivity to the overall balance of texture; the Orff class arranging a nursery rhyme senses the space between words. Complementarity is an essential principle of composition and improvisation—and dressing, cooking, and marriage as well!

An ear for aesthetic balance grows through practice and attention. This game (and similar activities) is a good starting point for a learning much deeper than simply memorizing names. By starting with an artistic premise, the game opens up to players of any age, cultural background, and musical experience. (I would love to play this game with Zakir Hussain, Bobby McFerrin, Yo Yo Ma, Tito Puente, and Keith Jarrett!)

GAME 8. SPELLING NAME

Skill: Audiation

Concept: Meter

Activities:
- Make a circle. All spell their names simultaneously, one letter per beat.
- Repeat, accenting the first letter: <u>C</u> h r i s <u>C</u> h r i s.
- Repeat, speaking the first letter and internalizing the others: <u>C</u> * * * * <u>C</u> * * * *
- Walk into the center of the circle and join with all those having names of the same number of letters; return to the original circle in new groups.
- Each group chooses one name from the group and all speak the first letter, gesturing to show the accent: three groups: Chris, Don, and Jennifer

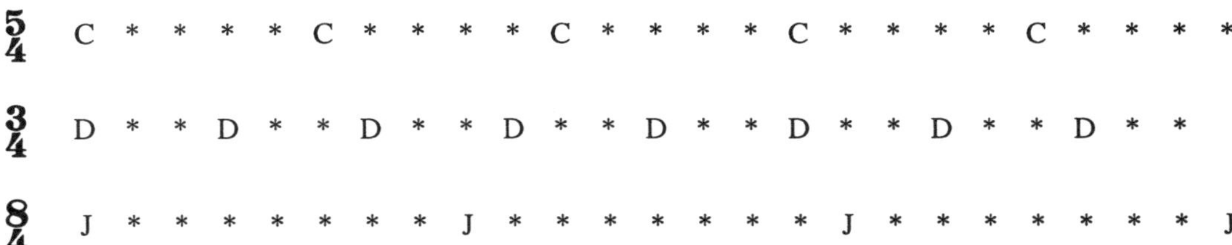

- Each group claps its first letter, improvises body percussion in the space of full name.

Variations:
- Transfer above to movement.
- Transfer to unpitched percussion.
- Transfer to pitched percussion, each group creating a pattern of one pitch per letter.

Comments:

This introduction to meter—the regular grouping of beats—keeps the music close to the language side of the brain and avoids abstract counting. The inherent variety of name lengths allows for a broader experience of meters than the usual twos, threes, and fours of most Western music. Names longer than six letters may choose to create secondary accents: **J** e n n i **f** e r **J** e n n i **f** e r.

This game requires a steady beat and skillful audiation to keep track of the large aural space between downbeats. Once mastered, exciting group textures will rise from the confluence and divergence of the accented letters. Once again, a simple idea moves us into interesting compositional territory normally reserved for "advanced" music study—polymeter, odd meters, and secondary accents.

Classroom teachers might adapt this technique of hooking spelling to beat, accent, and gesture for spelling difficult words.

GAME 9: SOUND OF FIRST LETTER

Skill: Vocal improvisation

Concepts: Character of each sound
Alliteration

Activities:

- All explore the sound of the first letter of their name, adding vowels to consonants (be, ba bay, bo, boo, etc.) and consonants to vowels (odi, ori, oli, omi, etc.).
- Walk into the middle of the circle expressing sound as above and find all those who share the same sound (not necessarily the same first *letter* but the same *sound*—Cindy joins Susan, Cathy joins Kate). Group together and return to the original circle. (As in previous games, "one of a kinds" group together.)
- Each group briefly presents its sound to make sure everyone is in the right group.
- Each group creates a short improvisation (based on its sound) which can be conversational, metered, or a combination of the two. (See GAME 5 for general rules of improvisation.)
- Learn everyone's name following the process outlined in GAME 6.

Variations:

- Repeat the above process using the <u>last</u> letter sound of each name: "Laur<u>a</u> Mar<u>a</u> Frid<u>a</u> Sar<u>ah</u>"
- Each group creates a movement improvisation based on its sound (deflating like balloons for <u>s</u>, popping like popcorn for <u>p</u>, etc.).

Comments:

When I asked my class to identify one of the principles in this game, a very sharp student replied, "Each sound has its own character." Beautifully put! To feel more at home in the world of language, we can imagine each sound as a unique character in an extended family and spend some time with them all—the percussive <u>p</u>, the mouthwatering <u>m</u>, the awesome <u>ah</u>, the crackling <u>k</u>, the sizzling <u>s</u>, and more. Learning the musical quality of each sound in the alphabet is like learning the sound of each instrument in a symphony orchestra. For the music student, it helps tune the ear to the language of music and its nuances of timbre—vital skills in songwriting, scat singing, and the setting of text; for the language student, it helps tune the ear to the music of language and leads to alliteration in poetry and prose.

Here, alliteration is the key associative memory trick for learning everyone's name—"Peter, Paul, Paolo, Penny, Jenny, Jasper, Jillian"—and we notice the loss of musicality when we arrive at the one-of-a-kind group—"Richard, Ken, Wolfgang, Abby."

GAME 10. NAME STORIES

Skill: Story improvisation

Concept: Polymeter

Activities:

- Group according to the first sounds as in GAME 9. If a group is larger than six, divide into smaller groups.

- Each group creates an ostinato with their names, accenting the first name in the series and accompanying it with a group gesture:

- The first person in the group tells the story of how she or he was named while the group continues speaking the ostinati softly and gesturing on the accent. The ostinati should be to a steady beat, providing a background texture while the storyteller speaks freely above. The speaker joins the ostinati when he or she is finished and the next person in the group tells his or her name story. (If the class is small enough, each group can perform one at a time. If this would take too long, all groups can perform simultaneously, telling stories within the groups.)

Variations:

- Select a group with three people, with four, and with five. Assign all other groups to join one of these three.

- All three groups perform their ostinati simultaneously to a common beat (accompanying with gesture as above). Volunteer storytellers step into the middle of the circle. When the narrators finish, the ostinati fade out:

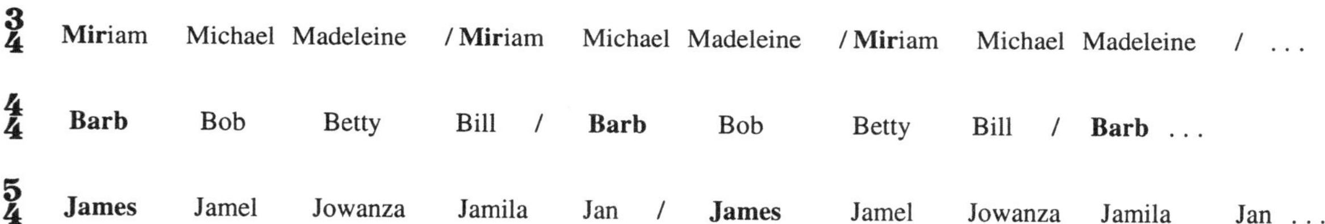

- Ostinati may be sung.

Comments:

I recently played this game with the staff at my school. Though I have known many of them for more than 20 years, it was the first time I heard the stories of how they were named. In the process of playing with them, I realized I didn't really know my own story! (I had some vague notion that I was named after Douglas MacArthur, but my mother subsequently informed me that she simply liked the way the g of Doug went with the g of Goodkin.)

The story of our name is a powerful piece of our personal history. It tells of our parents' hopes and aspirations for us before they knew who we were to become. Some names connect us to a spiritual affiliation (Mohammed, Krishna, Jesus), to a family history—notable aunts, uncles, grandparents—to a place (we named our first daughter Kerala after spending a marvelous five months in that state in southern India), to a mythical figure (we named our second daughter Talia after the Greek muse of Comedy and Poetry), to a name's meaning, to a hero or heroine. As the stories come out in this game, the presence of ancestors fills the room.

Musically, this game highlights the principle of background and foreground. The spoken ostinati provide a rhythmic and textural foundation over which the "melody" of the story soars. The contrast between the metered background rhythms and the unmetered foreground text makes for an intriguing musical setting. Such contrasts can be found in pieces as diverse as Charles Ives' "The Unanswered Question," Art Lande and Mark Isham's "The Melancholy of Departure," and Woodie Guthrie's "Talkin' Blues" recordings.

I first tried this game at a workshop in Iceland. All the groups spoke their parts with a beautifully sung speech natural to their singing culture while the soloist told her spirited story in the sonorous Icelandic language. Undistracted by the meaning of her words and unfamiliar with the names being chanted, the total effect was pure music to my ears. I have done this exercise many times since, but never with the exquisite musicality of its premiere Icelandic performance.

Game 11. Dramatic Alliteration

Skill: Dramatic improvisation

Concept: Alliteration

Activities:

• Form groups by first sounds as in GAMES 9 and 10. Each group writes a short poem, saying, or story based on its first sound:

"Betty and Bobby baked big bagels while bopping to the blues."

• Each group enacts its verse through miming the action of the composed text; everyone else tries to guess the poem. (This is difficult but worth the effort.) If they fail to guess correctly, the performing group reveals its verse.

Variations:

• Fold spoken version of the verse into the performance.

• Create a song based on the verse with supporting melodic ostinati derived from the text:

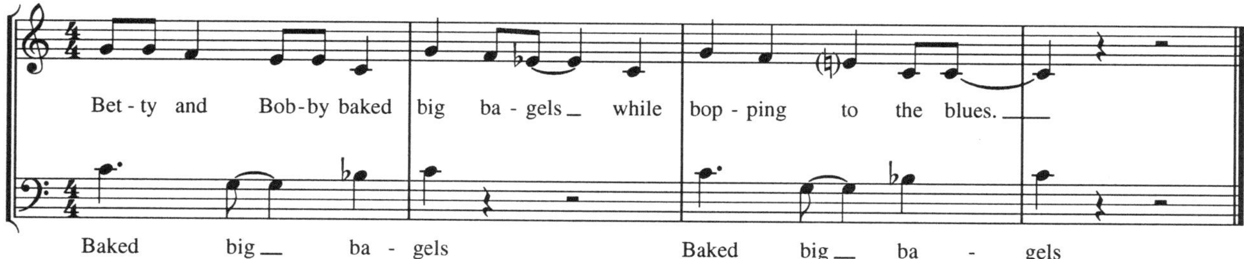

Comments:

The drama teacher might aim this exercise toward mime; the dance teacher might abstract the movements and move toward choreography; the language arts teacher might use this as a lead-in to alliterative poetry; the music teacher might emphasize composing with the text (as in variation 2). In any case, the result is always lighthearted fun. (Also a good substitute for Charades at your next party.)

Game 12. Name and Gesture

Skills: Self-reflection
Precise imitation and articulation

Concepts: Body language
Individuality
Articulation

Activities:

- All say their names one at a time while making a typical habitual gesture or posture (flipping hair out of face, pushing glasses up on nose, biting lip, folding arms across chest, etc.). Group echoes each name and gesture, with attention to precise imitation of voice quality and gesture.

- Repeat around circle, adding one at a time, until all gestures are memorized.

- Leader calls a name, group shows that person's gesture.

Variations:

- Go around the circle expressing each gesture without speaking the names.

- Small groups create a movement piece that combines the gestures in a sequence, with improvised or set movements connecting the gestures.

Comments:

This game requires a degree of self-reflection possible only with older children and adults. Although five-year-olds don't have enough awareness of self to identify an habitual gesture, they can play the game by simply creating a motion that goes with their name.

Here we are aiming for a higher level of knowing and a more personal level of sharing—an awareness of "clichés" in one's own body language and recognizing the same in others. The game suggests a body intelligence that speaks of who we are and invites the group to celebrate and amplify it. The group's precise attention to voice quality and gesture while imitating—tentative, confident, reserved, serene, boisterous—echoes back to each individual what he or she projects. A therapist might use this game as an opening to self-examination and analysis. A music teacher takes the offerings as raw material for aesthetic development, less concerned with *why* we scratch our nose and more with *how* we might do it larger, slower, or faster with sound effects.

GAME 13. RHYTHMIC NOTATION

Skill: Translating speech to spoken notation

Concept: Identifying duration values

Activities:

- Write students' names on the board from the following categories: one syllable (Sue), two syllables (Milo), three syllables (Jessica), and four syllables (Anabella). All names must begin on the beat (as in given examples). (Use names of other people in the school if needed to fill in the groups.)
- All pat a steady beat on their knees while reciting given names. (Students should be facing the board.) Explain the relationship of each name rhythm to the steady beat. (1 to 1, 2 to 1, 3 to 1, and 4 to 1.)
- Let students draw examples of these relationships on the board:

```
RHYTHM: ^   ^   ^   ^     ^ ^ ^ ^ ^ ^ ^ ^     ^ ^ ^ ^ ^ ^ ^ ^ ^ ^ ^ ^     ^^^^^^^^^^^^^^^^
  BEAT: *   *   *   *     *   *   *   *       *     *     *     *         *   *   *   *
```

- Write name rhythms on the board in standard notation:

Sue = ♩

Milo = * ♫

Jessica = ♪♪♪ (triplet, 3)

Anabella = ♬♬ (four sixteenth notes)

- Assign vocal syllables to each as follows:

Sue = ♩ = ta (pronounced *tah)*

Milo = ♫ = ta te (*te* pronounced *tay)*

Jessica = ♪♪♪ (triplet, 3) = ta ka ti (*ti* pronounced *tee)*

Anabella = ♬♬ = ta ka te ke (*ke* pronounced *kay)*

- Each chooses a name and recites the appropriate vocalization when teacher points to the name while patting a steady beat.

* As suggested in GAME 5, ♬ 𝄾 for Milo is more natural, but ♫ serves our goal of introducing beginning notation.

Variations:

• Volunteer writes a pattern of duration values, group translates to syllables and names:

Comments:

Alfred North Whitehead makes a useful distinction between three phases of education in his book The Aims of Education. The first he calls the "Stage of Romance," when "*. . . the subject matter has the vividness of novelty; it holds within itself unexplored connections with possibilities. . . .*" The second he calls the "Stage of Precision," when "*. . . width of relationship is subordinated to exactness of formulation. It is the stage of grammar. . . .*"

Our games until this point have been mostly in the "Stage of Romance," what my Orff teacher Avon Gillespie called "possibility teaching." With this game, we cross the line into the "Stage of Precision," setting names in standard notation. We won't stay long here; there already exists many clever techniques for introducing written notation. This book is aimed at awakening the child's intuitive musical thinking, for as Whitehead notes:

> *It is evident that a stage of precision is barren without a previous stage of romance; unless there are facts which have already been vaguely apprehended in their broad generality, the previous analysis is an analysis of nothing.*

Yet it is equally problematic to leave things fermenting in their romantic beginnings without giving the tools of precision for further development. I include this exercise simply to emphasize that it must be done and to give one way to begin the journey from the romance of art to the discipline of craft—and back again with renewed power of expression. Whitehead's third phase is the "Stage of Generalization," "*. . . a return to romanticism with the added advantage of classified ideas and relevant technique.*" These games live in the first stage, prepare the second, and should be revisited in the third.

The rhythmic syllables offered here are adapted from the French time-name system, one of several notational approaches used throughout the U.S. and Europe to teach rhythmic durations. It is an excellent extension of the previous games because:

- The connection between speech and rhythm is reinforced.
- The fact that Al, Lars, Tess, and Anne have the same relationship to the beat is represented by a single constant syllable—ta (which we will later identify as a "quarter note").
- Wedding that syllable to a notated figure connects the ear and eye, preparing the students for written notation.

This exercise serves as one of many possible introductions to this notational system. * The given examples—quarter, eighth, triplets, and sixteenth notes—show the range of basic values. Begin with quarter and eighth notes and add the others when appropriate.

* For a more detailed account of this system and discussion of how to handle syncopation, upbeats, half and whole notes, etc., see Some Great Music Educators, edited by Kenneth Simpson, Novello Press.

GAME 14. FIRST AND LAST NAME

Skill: Translating speech to rhythm

Concepts: Complementary rhythms
Combining monorhythm and polyrhythm

Activities:

- Each person speaks his or her first and last name to a steady beat; group echoes by clapping the speech rhythm. (Names may have to be repeated several times at the beginning.):

Cynthia: *Cynthia Marshall* Group:

Thomas: *Thomas O'Connery* Group:

- Group chooses two or more names that complement each other rhythmically (as above) and simultaneously recite names or express with body percussion. You may wish to write the notation on the board to provide a visual model of the complementary rhythms:

Cynthia Marshall:
Thomas O'Connery :

- Group chooses four names and places them in a sequence to create a rhythmic phrase:

Ko-ni-ko Nak-a-mu-ra, Ma-ri-lyn Du-pont, Fran-cis Spen-cer, A - li - sha Sims

- Some perform complementary rhythms of chosen names (Cynthia Marshall/Thomas O'Connery in the example above), others the above rhythmic phrase:

Variations:

- Create rhythmic phrases of different lengths or in different meters.
- Transfer all of the above to unpitched percussion.
- Transfer to melody in a pentatonic scale, sung, and/or played on Orff instruments.

Comments:

Now we have moved from the single word—our first name—to two words (or three, in the case of hyphenated last names). This is socially significant because we often have not learned the last names of our students (or classmates). Our last names carry a different piece of who we are: the larger identity of our ancestry. * When people speak their family names to the group, it creates a markedly different feeling in the air.

Musically, the first and last names give us longer and more varied rhythms to work with. By this point, the concept of complementary rhythms should be clear and students can be asked to make more conscious choices in their orchestration. (More practice at notation also aids this process.) Here the monorhythms and polyrhythms introduced in previous name games combine to form a more complex orchestration. By constantly revisiting basic concepts—complementary rhythms, rhythmic phrase, duration values, monorhythm, and polyrhythm—we build on a solid foundation and lead the student up the spiral of learning.

* Robert Bly criticizes our contemporary society's over-emphasis of first names in his book The Sibling Society: *"The first names make sense in a sibling way. The speaker doesn't want to imply by using your last name that your family is different from hers or his. To omit the last name is to say, 'Your ancestors are totally unimportant to us. You are a highly individualized individual floating in a bright ocean of individuals and we just love your particular essence.'"*

Game 15. Full Name and Birthday

Skills: Perform two rhythms simultaneously
Play, sing, and dance simultaneously

Concepts: Positive/negative space
Texture

Activities:

- All perform the following body percussion ostinato:
  pat knees–clap hands–touch neighbor's hand on left and right–clap hands
- Each recites first and last name and birthday in turn, fitting it into two cycles of the above patterns:

- All speak name and birthday four times, then clap it four times. Continue alternating speaking and clapping.
- Leader continues body percussion ostinato; group snaps first name, claps last name, pats birthday month, stamps birthday date (may pat floor with hands if seated).

- Play two elements and internalize the rest.

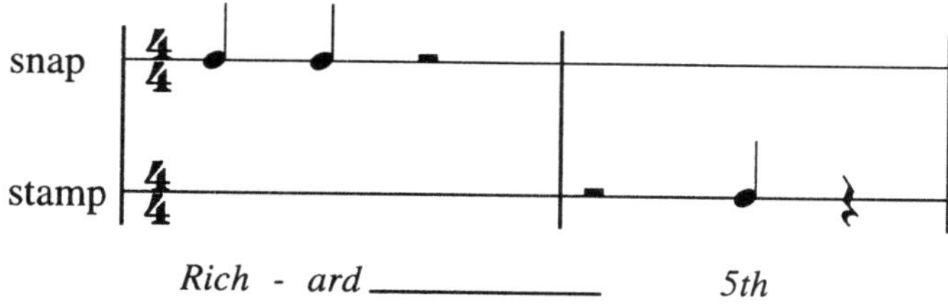

Variations:

- Play a version of the ostinato with one hand: pat–snap–chest–snap while patting name and birthday rhythm with the other; switch hands.

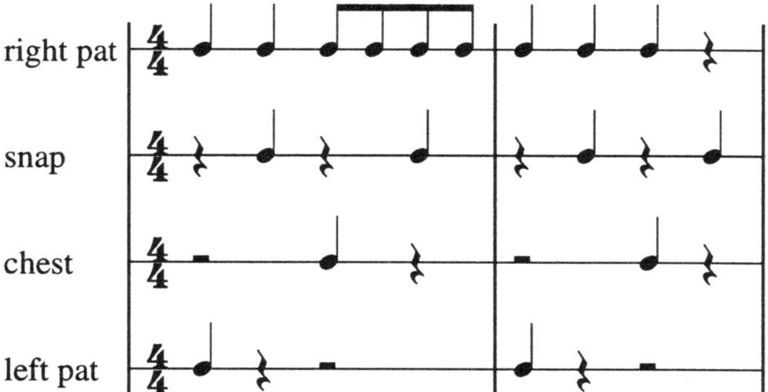

- Play again, switching to unpitched percussion, dividing the parts between four people (e.g.: pat = hand drum, snap = woodblock, chest = shaker, name and birthday = cowbell).
- Play on chosen words, move on remaining words. Half of the group moves, the other plays; switch.
- As above, improvising sung ostinati while moving.

Comments:

This game shifts us from "random" compositions to challenging rhythmic skill-building. We begin with two levels of rhythm. First we keep the body percussion ostinato while speaking our name rhythm. We then contrast spoken and clapped rhythm. From clapping, we change the texture of the overall rhythms by using different parts of the body. Audiation of some words thins out the texture even more. Then, by transferring some names to unpitched percussion, we move back from rhythmic skill building to "random" composition.

Extensions such as these are the heart and soul of "possibility teaching." Our small circle of mediums and materials—voice, body percussion, movement, percussion instruments, names, and birthdays—invites us to play with the possible combinations. Each one activates a different center of intelligence and has its own aesthetic quality. (Those who imagine we need state-of-the-art technology to ensure successful learning might be surprised by the unlimited possibilities that lie within our own bodies, voices, and imaginations—fertile ground to be cultivated before venturing into their extensions.)

Some of the variations are indeed demanding and would challenge even the most accomplished musician (try Variation 1!). The final variation is a beautiful example of the Orff ideal of playing, singing, and dancing simultaneously.

Game 16. Birthday Groups

Skills: Circle dance
Skipping (step-hopping)

Concept: ABC Form

Activities:

• Form a circle. Leader sings song below on the vocable "La" and dances with all imitating as follows:

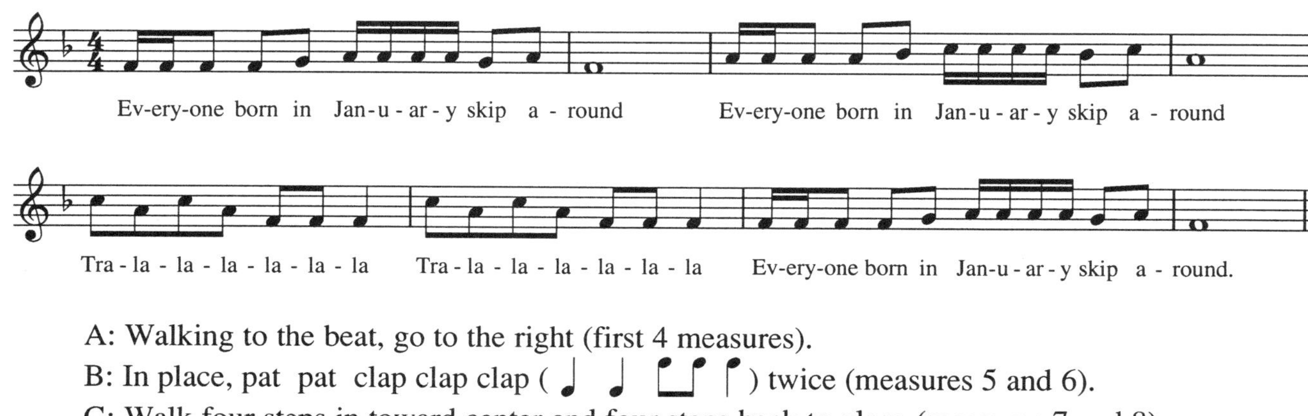

A: Walking to the beat, go to the right (first 4 measures).
B: In place, pat pat clap clap clap (♩ ♩ ♫ ♪) twice (measures 5 and 6).
C: Walk four steps in toward center and four steps back to place (measures 7 and 8).

• All sing the song with the words. Those born in the month named go to center and "skip around" (technically, step-hop, as the song is not in the 6/8 skipping meter) in the opposite clockwise direction. On the B section, all people skipping in the center meet and clap each other's hands on the clapping part. Return to original circle during the C section.

• After singing December, change words to "Everyone in the room skip around." In the B section, all who share the same birthday month find each other and skip together in the C section. At the end of the song, all return to original circle with their birthday group and arrange themselves in order, with January at one o'clock and December at twelve o'clock.

• Each group arranges itself chronologically by birth<u>date</u>.

• All perform a pat-clap; in turn, everyone announces her or his birthdate and group echoes.

• Ask these questions:
  • Which month has the most birthdays? The least?
  • Are there two or more who share the same birthday?
  • Do any people share the same date (1, 19, 30, etc.)?
  • Which date is the most common?

• All pat-clap, counting to 31. When birthdate number is called, all born on that date step forward.

Variations:

- Each group brainstorms and sings a song associated with their birth month. ("April Showers," "June Is Busting Out All Over," "See You in September," etc.)
- Each group mimes activities associated with their birth month—swimming, skiing, etc.

Comments:

The theme of birthdays and months is bursting with possibilities. Classroom teachers might graph the answers given to the previous questions, figure out the probabilities of shared birthdays in a random group of people, chant the months to the beat, make a list of things that come in twelves (12 hours on a clock, a dozen eggs, 12 Days of Christmas, 12 knights at King Arthur's round table, etc.), find poems about the months, write poems about the months, discuss what brings the change of seasons*, compare the variety of calendars, trace the origins of each month's name, make calendars in art class with drawings or prints for each month—indeed, the entire year's curriculum could be built around this theme!

Drama is one of the best vehicles for tying these threads together. "The Month Brothers," an Eastern European fairy tale found in Joanna Cole's collection Best-Loved Folktales of the World, is a perfect story to introduce the theme of the months. When my third-graders performed a version of this story, they began by researching many of the suggestions above. Some of that study was then incorporated into the play. The things they liked and disliked about each season found its way into the scripted dialogue, as well as parts of famous poems about the months; T.S. Eliot's, *"April is the cruelest month, breeding lilacs out of the dead land . . . ,"* William Wordsworth's *"Ye that pipe and ye that play, . . . feel the gladness of the May . . . ,"* and Robert Burns' *"My love is like a red, red rose, that's newly sprung in June. . . ."* The grand finale of the play as the poor mother and her children paid their annual visit to the Month Brothers was a rousing version of "Everyone Born in January."

Alfred North Whitehead said, *"You must not divide the seamless coat of learning."* Schools are infamous for dividing up that coat until it is shredded into a tangled knot of meaningless threads. Orff Schulwerk—and particularly its attention to drama—makes whole again what the daily round of schedule and subject has torn asunder.

*A recent poll taken at Harvard revealed that most graduates didn't know what made the seasons! (From video titled: *The Private Universe*. Merrill Ed. Products. ISBN 0-13-859646-8).

Game 17. Personal Favorite *

Skill: Sequential memory

Concept: Cumulative form

Activities:

- First person in the circle says his or her name and favorite _____. The blank could be food, color, book, musical style, school subject, musician, hero, animal, coffee blend, and so on. Group echoes back both pieces of information:

  Cheryl: *My name is Cheryl and I like sushi.*
  Group: *Her name is Cheryl and she likes sushi.*

- Second person says name and favorite. Group repeats the first and then the second.

  Wynton: *My name is Wynton and I like burritos.*
  Group: *Her name is Cheryl, she likes sushi; his name is Wynton, he likes burritos.*

- Continue as above, adding one at a time.

  Group: *Cheryl—sushi; Wynton—burritos; Justin—spaghetti, etc.*

- Go around the circle again reciting only favorite thing/person. Go again just reciting names.

- Use the two pieces of information to create a piece using any of the devices from previous games; e.g., singing one, clapping the other.

Variations:

- When appropriate, have students add a gesture, such as miming an instrument played by a favorite musician.

- When appropriate, have students share knowledge of their favorite thing, by briefly telling something about their favorite book, for example.

- Group people who share the same favorite thing and have them create something. For example, if musical style is the category, country music lovers work out a version of a country song, jazz lovers, a jazz song, and so on.

- Sing songs that are based on a cumulative form ("Rattlin' Bog," "A Hole in the Bottom of the Sea," "The 12 Days of Christmas," "Children Go Where I Send Thee") and dance dances that use the same principle (the folk dance "Seven Jumps").

Comments:

We have been learning a lot about each other through these games, from our birthday to the story of our naming. This game provides an open forum to reveal other parts of ourselves. What else might we want to know about our students? "Favorite pizza toppings" might be fun, but perhaps "heroes and heroines" gets us deeper under the skin of each student. Our choice of topic will change for each age group—favorite color for three-year-olds, favorite animal for seven-year-olds, favorite rock group for thirteen-year-olds, favorite car for seventeen-year-olds.

This game is an excellent way to introduce a thematic unit. I love to start my eighth-grade jazz study and adult jazz classes by asking for favorite jazz musicians. That question provides a wealth of useful information:

- I get a sense of the background and listening experience of each person.
- It introduces the names of some musicians we will encounter in our study.
- It includes the students in the information-gathering process.
- Occasionally, I learn of new musicians.
- It provides another associative memory hook—if I can't remember Sal, the mention of John Coltrane may help remind me.

I begin this game without a steady beat, but the group often settles into one.

* I thank my colleague Rick Layton for introducing me to this game.

Game 18. Rhymed Couplets

Skills: Verbal improvisation
Rhythmic improvisation

Concept: Phrase length

Activities:
• All perform simple pat-clap pattern while reciting this line:

"Hi, everybody, my name is ________."

• In turn, each recites line with his or her name. The entire group responds by improvising a rhyming line on the spot. (The result will sound chaotic as everyone comes up with a different line, but this method gives people a chance to try things out without being self-conscious.)

• In pairs, everyone creates a rhyming line for his or her partner. When all are ready, partners introduce each other to the group:

"Hi, everybody, his name is Fred,
He just woke up and got out of bed."

"Hi, everybody, her name is Elly,
She goes home every night and watches the telly."

After each pair of couplets, the entire group improvises body percussion for 32 beats. Return to pat-clap and the next partners speak.

Variations:
• During the improvisation, speaker goes into the center and mimes the action of the rhyme.

• Reverse above: speaker does the rhythmic improvisation, everyone else mimes the action.

• Substitute the children's song "Hey Lolly Lolly."

Comments:
This little game encourages the spontaneous rhyming that will help the students improvise blues or freestyle rap. The body percussion section helps develop the sense of aural space; the students must feel the length of the two couplets while performing the rhythmic improvisation. Amidst the main course of compositionally more nutritious offerings, this piece serves as a palate cleanser.

GAME 19. ICKY BICKY SODA CRACKER

Skills: Sensing phrase length
Maintaining two-level activity
Listening and recall

Concept: Phrase length

Activities:

- All recite poem while performing this clapping pattern: pat–clap–both hands out–clap:

- Perform clap pattern with a partner, touching index fingers on the word "you."

- Internalize the poem and walk around the room; take three jumps on "Who are you?" and immediately begin the clapping pattern with nearest partner. Continue alternating partner clap pattern (A section) with walking/jumping to find a new partner (B section).

- At leader's signal, stay with the last partner and learn a new game. The A section (recitation and partner clapping) remains the same. Instead of reciting and walking for the B section, one partner tells the other his or her name and as much information as possible while continuing the clapping pattern (to the beat or unmetered), ending after four clap patterns (16 beats). Return to the A section. Other partner tells autobiography for next B section. Return to the A section and stop.

- One at a time around the circle, each person tells the group what he or she remembers about the partner.

Variations:

- Anyone not finding a new partner by "you" is "out," but continues to participate during subsequent B sections by expressing the rhythm of the rhyme by clapping or on a percussion instrument.

- During partner "biography" game, continue the A-B cycle, giving new information each time.

Comments:

I don't tell my students ahead of time to remember what their partners tell them. When it comes time to share, many are surprised by my question and sheepishly confess, "I wasn't really listening!" This is a good time to slip in a reminder that they're responsible for listening *every* moment of the music class. Without listening, there's no music!

It's quite a challenge to tell your story while keeping the clapping play going and staying in the 16-beat form. (Don't try this with the little ones!) It's also interesting to feel the difference between speaking tied to the beat or letting it flow freely over it—a good introduction to different ways of setting melody.

With this game, we have moved from the single name to full-fledged rhymes and crossed into the next phase of the music-language connection. My book, A Rhyme in Time (BMR08006) © 1997 Warner Bros. Publications, ISBN 0-7692-1512-2, explores this territory through games and improvisational structures based on nursery rhymes. Having played some of these games, we're ready to continue our musical journey with more knowledge of our fellow travelers and how we work together as a group. Before we get off the name train, we have one more stop.

GAME 20. RUMPELSTILTSKIN

Skill: Dramatic interpretation

Concept: Synthesis of previous material

Activities:

• Tell/read the story of Rumpelstiltskin.

Brief synopsis: A miller boasts to a king that his daughter can spin straw into gold. The king locks her up in a room and demands that she do so by morning. A little man appears to the distraught daughter and offers to do the spinning in exchange for her necklace. When the king sees the gold the next morning, he demands the same the next night. Again, the little man appears and does the work in exchange for a ring. The next day, the king offers to marry the daughter if she can succeed in this task one more night. That night when the little man appears, the daughter has nothing more to offer him. He requests her first-born child and she agrees. She marries the king and one year later, gives birth to a child. The little man appears and demands his payment. She pleads for mercy and he agrees to cancel their bargain if she can guess his name in three days. She thinks of every name imaginable and sends servants far and wide to find every name they can. She fails to guess correctly the first two days and is in despair, when a huntsman reports that he came upon a little man in the forest singing this song:

"Brew today, tomorrow bake
After that the child I'll take,
And sad the queen will be to lose it.
Rumpelstiltskin is my name
But luckily nobody knows it."

The queen thanks the huntsman and, after trying the last name on her list, guesses "Rumpelstiltskin." The little man flies into a rage, grabs his foot, and tears himself in two.

• Dramatize the story and incorporate one or more of the name games. Some possibilities:

* Use some of the games with polyrhythmic ostinati (GAMES 3, 7, 14, 15) to perform on unpitched percussion while the little man spins the wheel. (An upside down tricycle makes a good spinning wheel.)

* Use other name games for scenes of servants seeking names. This minor part of the story can become the center of the drama. One servant enters a village and assembles the people to find out their names. They sit in a circle and say their names one at a time around the circle. The servant, trying to remember them all, asks them to do it again to a steady beat, as in GAME 2. In another village, another servant does the same, this time grouping them by syllables as in GAMES 5 and 6. In yet another village, another servant does the same, this time grouping by first letter, as in GAME 9. Finally, another servant uses rhyme to remember, as in GAME 18.

This form is perfect for a cross-grade performance (or cross-class in the case of two or more classes per grade); each class represents a "village" and showcases one of the name games.

* Create a dream sequence for the queen using whispered, overlapping ostinati as in GAME 10.

* Create a setting for Rumpelstiltskin's rhyme, offsetting the text by drawing from the students' experiences with complementary rhythm.

Variation:

- Research, collect, and/or perform other stories that have to do with naming. (The story "Anansi and the Secret Name" in the book Patakin by Nina Jaffe, Henry Holt & Co., offers a nicely contrasting story from a different culture.)

Comments:

Carl Orff's genius lay in his synthesis of art forms and is best seen in drama. This Grimm Brothers fairy tale provides a perfect opportunity to synthesize the activities in this book, moving a simple name from exercise to piece to dramatic performance—the "final exam." Along the way, there is much assessment that can (and should) be made regarding mastery of musical skills and understanding of musical concepts. Yet the most important assessment is not the judging of each child's progress, but the communal experience of creating, practicing, and sharing through performance.

The simple suggestions made here reveal much of the spirit of Orff-Schulwerk. Instead of using a pre-packaged script, the teacher imagines how these games might be used to enact the story and how the story might serve to gather the games. Once the teacher begins the dreaming, the creative forces begin to gather. (Some might begin with the children's dreaming, but my sense is that the teacher must first set the process in motion and *then* include the children's ideas as they work with the material.) When the work begins, it often takes on its own momentum, offering ideas and directions to which both teacher and students should respond.

Here we arrive at the essence of the Schulwerk—the spinning of straw into gold. From the raw material of names and a circle of people, we begin spinning out ideas and working them with our hands. Some are so fragile they snap, others bunch and coil, and some hit that rhythmic stride where the tension is just right and gold emerges. Much of our work is attention to details—the right postures, rhythms, fingerings, the skills of our craft. Yet our story suggests that skills and techniques alone are not enough—we need the help of that strange little man who lives beneath our conscious attention and intention. He will demand a price—the various sacrifices that artists and music teachers make—and he will ultimately asked to be named. "The Muse," "Intuition," or "Inspiration" are possibilities, but somehow too vague to fulfill the bargain. Each one of us must name our own guiding spirit. When we do, it will tear itself in two, no longer needed as a separate figure but now an indelible part of ourself.

TEACHER'S NOTES

TEACHER'S NOTES

TEACHER'S NOTES

TEACHER'S NOTES

DOUG GOODKIN teaches music and movement to children between three years old and the eighth grade at The San Francisco School, where he has taught since 1975. He is an internationally recognized practitioner of Orff-Schulwerk, teaching Orff courses throughout North America, Europe, and Australia. He is the director of the Mills College Orff Certification Course in Oakland, CA, and teaches his own summer course on jazz and Orff-Schulwerk.

Doug has published numerous articles on Orff in contemporary culture and is an author of the Macmillan/McGraw-Hill textbook series *Share the Music*. He is a founding member of the Orff-based adult performing group Xephyr. Doug is known for his innovative application of Orff-Schulwerk across various disciplines, particularly language arts, jazz, and multicultural music.